An Exciting Visit to the Farm House

Long Forgotten
Children's Adventure

Series - *Children's Nature Quest*

Author
M Borhan

From
Big 6 Publishing

Pencil Sketch of
a Farm House from Middle Ages

Inside the Farmhouse Complex
Hut 2
Front Hut 1
Entrance Gate
Today we shall take you to such a lovely Farmhouse to visit...

The Farmhouse

Farmers, Families or Guests stay here in the whole agricultural setting...

A Farmhouse has been one of the best places to visit for families in modern times to enjoy agriculture and get rejuvenated from Workloads, Busy Life and connect to agriculture, farm life, experiencing natural seasons....

Barns or
Sheds
Backyard
Shed
Inside
Shed
Soon, after the sunrise, the cows' herd are taken to the front yard...

shed1
Southern Yard
Joined Cow-Sheds
shed2
After the Sun goes a little up, the cows from the Joined Cow-Sheds are brought in the daylight to roam and move...

Outside
Crops Field
Soon before noon, the cows are brought
out to the outside field-grassland; where
the cows start grazing...

Vast
Grass Field
Then the cows move everywhere in the grassland for finding the most tender green grasses while enjoying sunshine...

After a while, the cows are brought back to the sheds, and it is time for some special dairy cow-food called-Total Mixed Ration. It is essential in their cow feed along with grasses !

Bathing Shed
After grazing and feeding, the Cows are ready for another adventure... at the backyard-shed, a specialized bathing small pond is ready for the cows to be washed properly...

So, this is the final destination, the cows have been grazed and washed properly till now for a healthy milking...
The cows are milked with specialized equipment directly without any direct human interventions...
Milk Shed

Now, all the Milk collected are taken away...
Milk Shed Side
Yeah! That's how we get the best dairy milk and products directly from the Farmhouse Complex !

Outside the Farmhouse Complex, the sheep also graze, but the flock of the sheep spend more time grazing on the pastures! Most of the time the flock remain very close to each other unlike the cows' herd.
Vast
Grass Field

Inside
Grass Field
Fence
While some sheep are grazing, some farm men
shave some sheep and collect wool from them,
it's called Shearing; and the removed wool, known
as Fleece, is collected after shearing.

North Side
Sheep Shade
After Wool Collection, the shaved
Sheep are brought back to the
shed by a Farm Man...

Sunset on North Side Sheep Shade
At Sunset, the Sheep flock is brought back...
In the yard, they are left for some time...

Southern
Yard
Some Cows are still outside to enjoy
the beauty of the night of moonlit sky.

Night Scene outisde Farmhouse Complex
Yeah! There are young kids, who come from neighboring area to enjoy the Farmhouse Complex's Night Beauty...

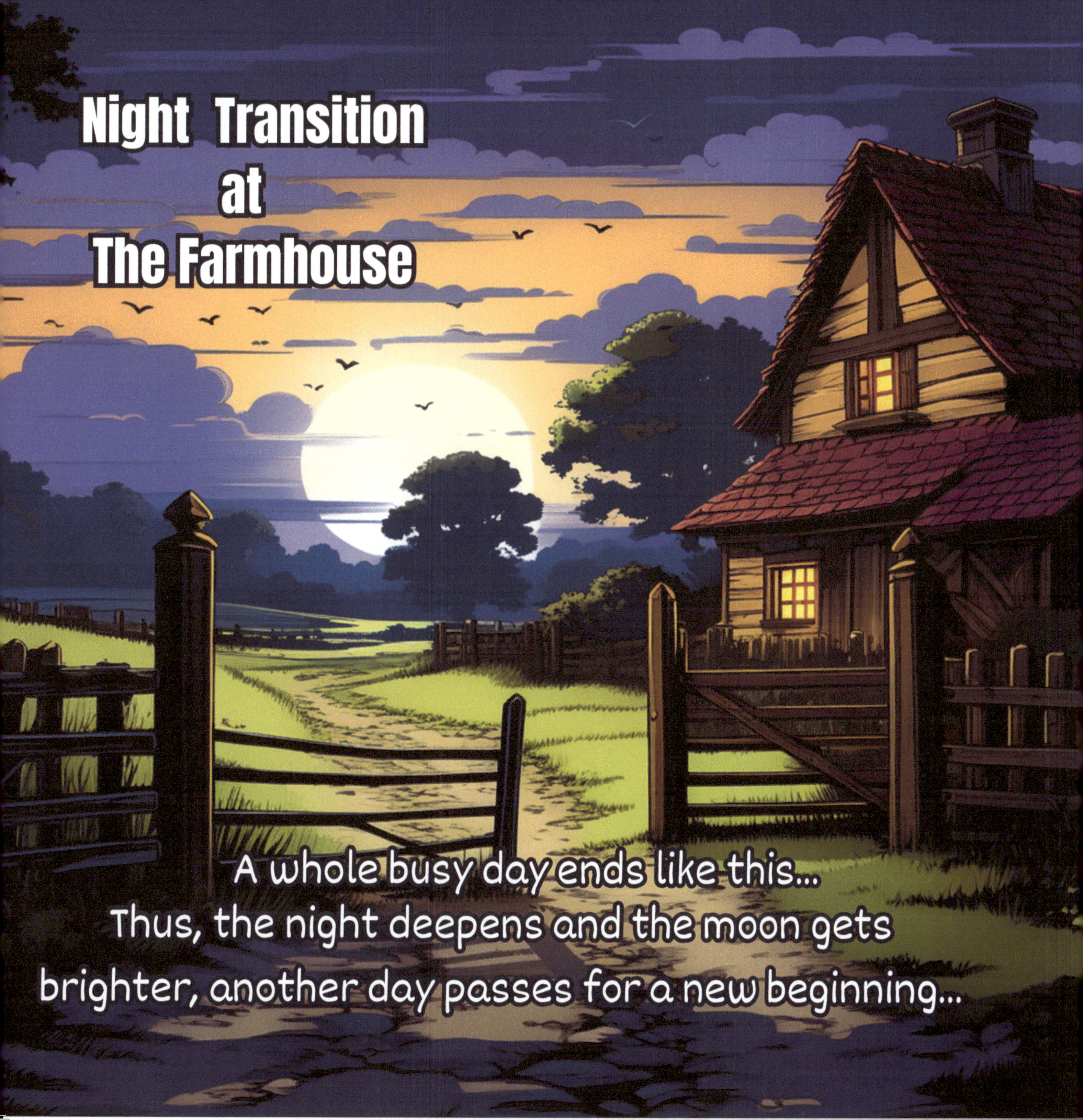

Night Transition
at
The Farmhouse
A whole busy day ends like this...
Thus, the night deepens and the moon gets
brighter, another day passes for a new beginning...

Sunrise at Southern Yard
A new day, new beginning... some cows wake up as early as the sun rises! That's how it all goes on in a farmhouse...

Grab Other Exciting Books

Book Series: Children's Knowledge Quest

Book Series: Grizzly Bear Series

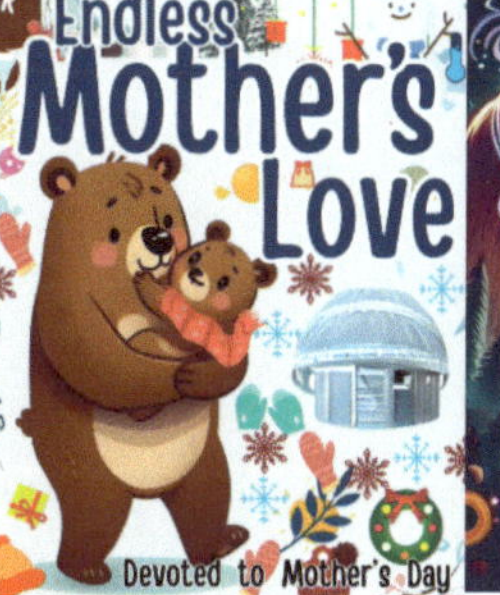

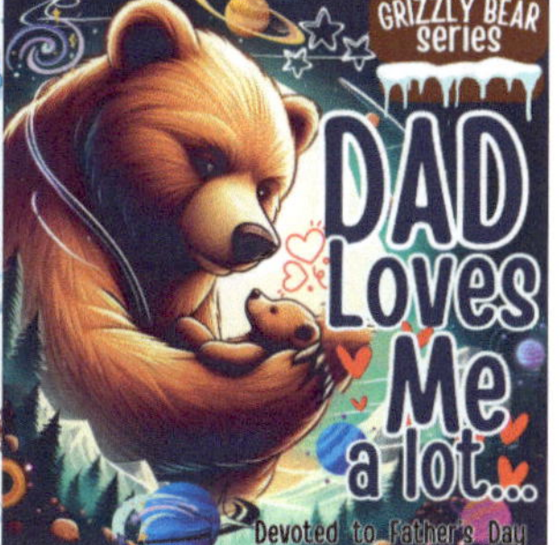

Other Series: Mixed Categories

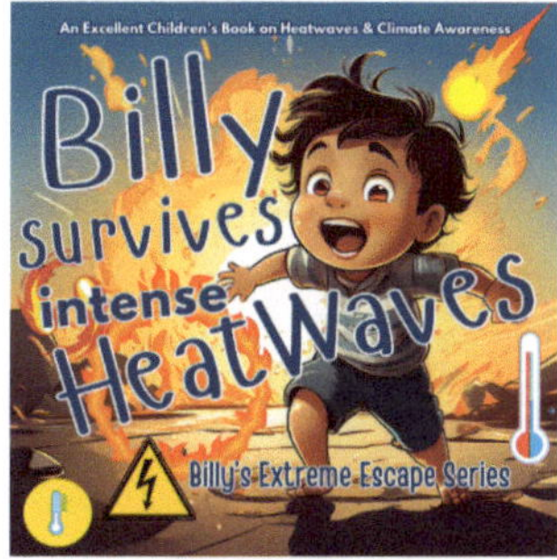

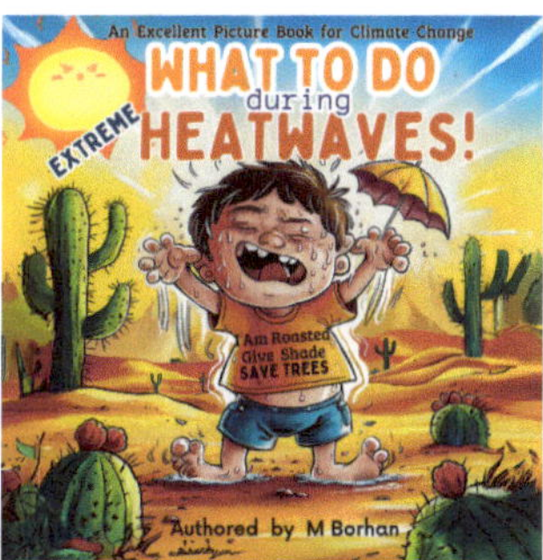

Instagram

Scan QRs, Follow & Like us

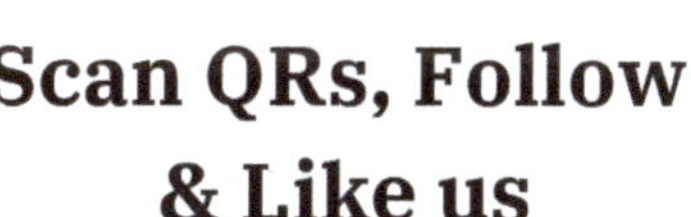

Pinterest

Tiktok

www.ingramcontent.com/pod-product-compliance
Lightning Source LLC
Chambersburg PA
CBHW041638110726
48005CB00002B/642